THE DIFFICULT DAYS

THE LOCKERT LIBRARY
OF POETRY IN TRANSLATION

Advisory Editor: John Frederick Nims

For other titles in the Lockert Library
see p. 81

THE
DIFFICULT
DAYS

Roberto Sosa

TRANSLATED BY
Jim Lindsey

PRINCETON UNIVERSITY PRESS

Copyright © 1983 by Princeton University Press
Published by Princeton University Press, 41 William Street,
Princeton, New Jersey 08540
In the United Kingdom: Princeton University Press,
Guildford, Surrey

Library of Congress Cataloging in Publication Data will be
found on the last printed page of this book

ISBN cloth 0-691-06583-7
paper 0-691-01407-8

The Lockert Library of Poetry in Translation is supported by a
bequest from Charles Lacy Lockert (1888-1974)

This book has been composed in Linotron Sabon
Clothbound editions of Princeton University Press books are
printed on acid-free paper, and binding materials are chosen for
strength and durability. Paperbacks, although satisfactory for
personal collections, are not usually suitable for library rebinding.

Printed in the United States of America by
Princeton University Press
Princeton, New Jersey

CONTENTS

v

INTRODUCTION

"A poem or a story could help civilize those who govern;
that's why we need governors who read"

Two Interviews with Robert Sosa

From the magazine *Plural* (Mexico City), May, 1982:

Roberto Sosa was born in 1930 in the village of Yoro (where, in his own words, "it rains fish and airplanes"), in Honduras ("that enormous cultural pothole in Central America"). He is one of the most serious and prolific living Honduran authors and his work has received awards in his own country and abroad.

Among his works are *Caligrams* (1959), *Walls* (1966), *The Sea Inside* (Juan Ramón Molinas Award, Honduras, 1967), *The Poor* (Adonais Award, Spain, 1967), *A Brief Study of Poetry and Its Creation* (1969), and *A World For All Divided* (Casa de las Américas Award, Cuba, 1971). His poetry has been translated into French, German, Russian, and, most recently, English.

Sosa has served as juror in the literary competitions *Miró* (Panama, 1976), *Casa de las Américas* (Cuba, 1979), *Ruben Darío* (Nicaragua, 1980) and others. For eight years now he has edited the magazine *Presente* (a review of Central American arts and letters), he was director of the University of Honduras Press, he is a member of the Honduran Academy of Language, and he currently is president of the Honduran Journalists' Union.

Plural conducted the following interview with the Honduran poet during a visit of his to Mexico. The interviewer is Roberto Bardini, an Argentine journalist specializing in Central American themes. He spent several years in Honduras as preparation for his recent book, *Connection in Tegucigalpa*.

vii

BARDINI: To warm to the subject, why don't you tell us a little about your early education; your infancy, adolescence, and youth; how you earned a living non-literarily; who your friends and enemies are; where you have been and what you have won; and anything else that occurs to you.

SOSA: I completed my early education in the little village of Yoro, that has been made famous by the rain of fish that falls in its environs (this phenomenon still has not been investigated scientifically; most people who hear about it for the first time smile slightly and make gestures of incredulity . . . justifiably, of course).

I've worked at several occupations to earn honorably my frijoles, tortillas, books, and music. From puberty to my second childhood I've sold bread, measured heights, wrote a poem or an editorial for a magazine or newspaper, or directed some journalistic endeavor.

Some of my awards have been non-literary. Two stand out. A primary school in Tegucigalpa, that before boasted the name of John F. Kennedy, was renamed for me. It has to do with a cultural recuperation. And a little street in Yoro now goes by my name. These two things have led me to feel a greater responsibility to the society that has honored me in this manner in my lifetime.

Friendship has a special meaning for me. A friend is someone one chooses as a brother. To travel and to think, and to know a friend is waiting for us, produces a feeling of security and confidence and happiness.

I know some countries of this continent and some of the Old World. It's true that "to travel is to reform oneself." Strange, brutal, and marvelous people get together and get to know each other. The first big city I became acquainted with was Mexico City, in 1963. I was impressed by the noise and the lights of six in the afternoon, and the Aztec multitude kicked and spit upon by the most lucid bourgeoisie of the continent, a bourgeoisie defended by a certain intellectuality (anti-?) situated "far from God and near the United States." That was eighteen years ago. Have things changed?

I have no enemies of quality and at times I think that's a pity. Most of my enemies, those I know, are intranscendentalists. To tell the truth, I have seen seven or eight intermediate enemies, full of hate (literary hate, which is no less corrosive than political hate, nor less refined) from the bottom of their glances to the tips of their gray hairs. I've never answered attacks except obliquely. It's a good practice. The attack exhausts itself and disappears, attacker and all. The poisoner drinks his own poison.

BARDINI: What can you tell us about Central America as a place for poetry? Does a Honduran literature exist?

SOSA: For whatever reason, Central America is definitely a place for poetry. Miguel Angel Asturias affirmed that the origin of this condition is in the light. The anthologists (read "fadologists") of poetry have taken a long time to represent the Honduran chapter and have confined it to modernism: Juan Ramón Molina and Froylan Turcios. The confectioners of almanacs have gone even further, have altered names, birthdates, biographies, bibliographies, and the rest.

BARDINI: What poets have most influenced the Hondurans? What weight, for example, have Pablo Neruda, César Vallejo, and Ruben Darío had?

SOSA: Darío, as you know, created a zone of influence in Honduras, wide enough that he still has imitators, including imitators of his decadent style. Neruda and Vallejo are key names in the poetic affairs of my country, although to tell the truth, the Chilean (Neruda) wove and unraveled in material of influence. On the other hand, at a continental level and in unclear circumstances, a whole army of poets disappeared along the Nerudan Way.

BARDINI: Does an official cultural policy exist in Honduras?

ix

SOSA: There exists no definite cultural policy on the part of the Honduran State. There never has. From the looks of it, that sector of the life of the country does not now nor has it ever interested them. Not too long ago a Ministry of Culture was created, but its work in that sense is remote and serves only to sustain the most anticultural bureaucracy that ever existed.

Honduras is maybe the only country in Latin America that has no Faculty of Humanities. And this absence in the Honduran educational system signals an enormous shortcoming in the formative process of its intellectuals—a term to be understood here in its widest sense—who, naturally, have been condemned to solitary study, without discipline. It has created a critical shortage in the supply of analytical, critical, and organized intellectuals. This doesn't mean there are only uncritical intellectuals. No. There are serious and honest intellectuals, but not in the measure and proportion that ought to exist in a country like ours, that needs responsible leaders.

BARDINI: What are the relations between the government and the intellectuals then, since there is no official cultural policy? Are there writers assimilated by the military regimes?

SOSA: The writers and the military governments have never maintained in Honduras—in any country, I think—very good relations to speak of. There are, of course, some intellectuals who have been—and will be again at a moment's notice—at the service of every military dictatorship. They are employed in the diplomatic services, as "ideological bodyguards" in the mass media, or as speechwriters. These last we call "Walt Disneys" because they make animals talk. They are gentlemen who live very well, dress very well, dispense drawing room ironies and laugh like hyenas, all full of grease, from overseas.

The intellectuals who assume denunciatory positions, on the other hand, are labeled "communists," "useless idiots," expressions that on the lips of the representatives of repression and of the "men of letters" of the Right have a bitter, slighting flavor.

BARDINI: Faced with that situation, which isn't much different from that of the rest of Latin America, what position do the Honduran intellectuals take? Are they organized, militant, do they respond?

SOSA: Honduran writers, and in general anyone related to the arts, are not integrated in blocks either national or international. The individualistic character of the Honduran has been pointed out as the principal element in this state of affairs. Intellectuals have arrived at the Left by way of sympathy and some have decided to militate (here this word loses its usual uniform) in the revolutionary ranks for reasons of conscience. Nevertheless, it should be pointed out that it isn't simple to belong to a Left like the Honduran, divided, subdivided, and subdividing itself. But I should make it clear that those Honduran intellectuals not glorified by the political power of the right, those who occupy key positions, demonstrate a pure attitude in the face of the shame and corruption of the State, and they do it by means of the poem, the story, the novel, the journalistic essay, and the drama.

For Central American writers there is no road left but to be in favor of the oligarchies or against them. To many intellectuals it has fallen to take arms to defend the ideas enclosed in their poems. Many pay with their lives in tragic ways, like the Guatemalan Otto René Castillo, who was burned alive by the military that unlawfully holds power in Guatemala. Central America is in flames. The list of the disappeared continues to grow with the names of consequential persons.

In Honduras, meanwhile, we are experiencing the slow but sure approach of political repression. All you need do is pick up the newspapers and read the wire stories of the international agencies to verify what I'm saying. The level of repression expands, the range of choices shrinks. The assassination of leftist leader Tomás Nativí, the disappearance of university students like Manfredo Velázquez, the kidnapping of economist Virgilio Carías, lend strength to these reports.

In other walks of life there also has been repression. Journalistic activity, for example, though the press is free, is limited in practice by the criteria of the owners of the media of communication and by the enforcement of medieval laws. Elsewhere, painstaking searches are carried out by sea, land, and air customs charged with detecting "subversive literature," "communist books."

BARDINI: They say Honduras is "a land of poets." What "antidotes" to this state of things are they generating? Do literary groups exist? Currents? Tendencies? That is to say, is there an organized intellectual effort?

SOSA: There have been poets in Honduras at every stage of its history, though not in the quantity announced by some. It's not true that my country is "a land of poets." Outside of some five names, the rest are stuck—maybe forever—in the purgatory of promise.

As for the lack of an official cultural policy, or the difficulties of creating, procreating, and surviving, or the internal political situation, which worsens by the day, there are for the moment, unfortunately, no "antidotes." There have existed groups of an episodic character, bearing the names of writers and poets. It seems that Hondurans dedicated to artistic creation don't like the idea of forming a nucleus. Maybe, as was said, this is due to a residual individualism of action that lives on inside them.

Nevertheless, without the previous baptism of a title, the intellectuals and poets (and isn't the poet, perhaps, an intellectual by antonomasia?) group themselves according to their position in the world. We have groups that clash, that envy each other. These situations are provoked, I think, by the narrow provinciality of Tegucigalpa, by some slow deviations that led us off the track forty years ago. That is to say, intranscendence, pure and simple.

From the magazine *Alcaraván* (Tegucigalpa), July, 1981:

SOSA: . . . I'd like right now to cite an expression of Sartre's woman, whose name I can't remember . . .

ALCARAVÁN: Simone de Beauvoir.

SOSA: She said that to be an intellectual in Honduras is to be a hero. . . . It's been said somewhere that miserable countries produce great poetry, and I believe that, in part, that statement is true. It's worthwhile to point out that, in the case of Nicaragua, another extremely backward country—luckily on the road today to cultural advancement—you come up with a Ruben Darío. In Honduras we have the likes of Juan Ramón Molina. It goes so far, even, that sometimes the economic apogee is not related with the quality of the literary production.

ALCARAVÁN: In Nicaragua, under the Somoza dictatorship, while every manifestation of social and economic progress was being liquidated, there was permitted (by a negative relationship) a great overall growth both in the quantity and quality of the poetry.

SOSA: That's so. The dictatorship served precisely to produce a literature of great quality. The questioning, the ferocious criticism aimed at the government, gave rise to a valid literature.

ALCARAVÁN: In the case of Honduras, we could recall the time of Carías. What effect did his dictatorship have on our arts and letters?

SOSA: It's very peculiar, and of great interest, that this dictatorship produced no great works. All the poetry surrounding Carías is pamphletary, without artistic quality. No pamphlet is artful. We have here, then, an inverse phenomenon to that of Nicaragua. While the dictatorship there served to support a work of quality, in Honduras it did not. Here the works were patronized by the dictatorship, which is to say some

xiii

writers wrote their work in exile, an exile made propitious by the dictatorship.

I believe there's a need to go deeper into this problem of power monopolized and taken to its extremes, as occurred with Carías. There are some friends of mine I'm always talking to, especially the narrators, and I make the case to them that there exists a lack of preoccupation with taking on the theme of the dictatorship in Honduras, and that it could happen, at any time, that some foreign writer could come in here and get the facts and put together a great novel. Why can't our own narrators put it together? We've had competent narrators. We had a rich vein in the period of Carías.

ALCARAVÁN: In that sense, it could be said that the dictatorship of Carías was a "novel without novelists."

SOSA: It was an epic of horror in sixteen volumes, written in blood.

ALCARAVÁN: The Carías situation somehow dovetails with that of our own day and age. Somehow it seems as if the official culture continues here with the same profile as the official culture then: that rural face, exactly as backward and undeveloped. . . .

SOSA: And underdeveloping!

ALCARAVÁN: Besides which we have a ministry that is coming to be a privilege purely external and apparent. At bottom, not the least advance has been made in the manner of dealing, on the part of the State, with matters of art and literature. Isn't that so?

SOSA: It seems to me that we are living a sort of cultural neo-Caríism. A neo-Caríism more uniform, more technical, more subtle, but still Caríism. There's the same darkness, the same narrownesses, the same cultural misery. What's more, it seems to me to be becoming even more shameless in its treatment of our national culture.

ALCARAVÁN: Carías passed on, but Caríism stayed alive in hiding. It manifests Carías' own luck. He was the only one of the great Central American dictators who was able to die peacefully at home, contrary to Somoza or Hernández Martínez.

SOSA: You could say that Carías is governing us from the grave. I read somewhere that he adored birdsong, and that while he listened to the birds he often ordered an assassination or an imprisonment.

ALCARAVÁN: Concerning the official sector, what opinion do you have about the cultural politics of our present-day government? Tell us something about the National Book Commission—the judging of the National Awards, for example.

SOSA: From the looks of it, the National Book Commission is not seriously intent on publishing anything. I haven't seen or heard of a single editorial program that's ready to be put into practice. As for the mechanisms of judging the National Awards, everyone knows that the officials in charge have no selective criteria. In recent years, for example, these awards have been given to people completely foreign to art, to social concerns, to any serious work.

ALCARAVÁN: What do you think ought to be the response of writers and artists independent of the official culture when those organs promote or publish names or works lacking even a minimum of quality?

SOSA: There ought to at least be a protest, some opposition. But I've seen nothing of the sort, except for the protest some of us writers signed when the 1980 National Literature Award was given to Mr. Oscar A. Flores, who already had departed the world of the living. In general, conformism and indifference are the rule, as if to all the world it's the same if they give an award to this person or that, including when the person receiving the award is nothing but the merest personification of the anticulture.

ALCARAVÁN: It turns the whole scale of values upside down.

SOSA: It's a confusion of values, to put it another way. Pure confusion. Nobody distinguishes one thing from another. If a person reads the newspapers, he finds infinite congratulations, for instance from the official diplomatic corps of our country, for whatever character has received an award, even though it's obvious they have no idea why he's receiving it.

ALCARAVÁN: Obviously, then, it's not enough in our medium to make a work well. It's also necessary to make an extra-literary effort to unmask the disorienting effects of the so-called "official culture." It would seem, then, to impose an extra task, one almost didactic, pedagogic.

SOSA: Here, for example, there are groups of people you never heard of, nor where they came from, who aren't backed by a serious work, a work established by just criticism, who suddenly spring up like some species of sacred cows.

ALCARAVÁN: It's evident that in Honduras there are more poets than narrators. I wonder if that's a trait peculiar to our literature?

SOSA: It's universal, really. Apparently it's easier to write poetry than prose. Every budding youth that falls in love, the first thing he does is write verses to his loved one, and since they are dictated by feeling, by emotion, he commences to fill reams without rhyme or reason. And if also he is eulogized by some critic, he comes automatically to "enrich the national bibliography," as we say. It follows that there are being created, by the irresponsibility of the critics, a lot of unnecessary "poets." Why do we have 150 poets in Honduras? I say 150 because that's how many appear in the "General Index of Honduran Poetry." As if we were classical Greece!

ALCARAVÁN: Another theme we haven't touched on, and that seems to us very important, is the evolution of your own poetry.

SOSA: I could start by speaking of my poetic prehistory, of what I read as a youth, of my isolation. I was born in a town where it rains fish, yes, fish fall from the sky (foreigners tell me this is a story invented by García Márquez). There, when I was fourteen years old and in the fifth grade, I first read some real writers, such as Darío and Molina. It was my first contact with poetry. After that I fell, as one falls in those towns, into an absolute void of literature: there was nothing to read. After a while I read Juan de Diós Peza. Also I remember a book that my father bought me, the first book I read all the way through. It was a book by Amado Nervo, *Interior Gardens*, and I learned it by memory. I had a fantastic memory. Everything I read I learned by memory. That book of Nervo enabled me to know a real poet, a poet accomplished and complete, as Nervo was in his time and in his context.

Many years later, here in Tegucigalpa, I came into contact with vanguardist poetry. I remember how non-modernist poetry, the intellectualized poetry of poets like Eduardo Carranza, put me in a daze. It was unfamiliar to me and it produced in me a strange sensation of acceptance and rejection. In those circumstances I began to write verses, a little on the sly, in private, and you show those verses to someone else so that they'll say, "That's good" or "That's bad" or simply "That is drivel, you ought to dedicate yourself to something else." Till you meet up with another person of higher quality, of greater knowledge, who says to you, "This position you take, this poetry you are making, has been being made for years by thousands of poets in Spain, in Argentina, in Chile, in Guatemala. But if you follow this other road of saying things simply and without refinement, that is your road." That person was Andrés Morris, who showed me a route to a style that let me write books like *The Poor* and *A World For All Divided*, and some poems of *Walls*, that have already the germ of that way of saying things simply, stripped, without rhetoric.

ALCARAVÁN: How do you see the evolution of your poetry, this successive stripping down?

SOSA: The first book I published, whose title I copied from Apollinaire, was *Caligrams*. At last I could see myself in print. Print has a very special mystery: it uncovers all kinds of mistakes. While the work is in manuscript, you can't view it objectively. It's not until it's published that you start to say, "That's bad," "That was not fit to be published." Then comes the criticism, at times terrible, cruel. People appear who dismiss us as poetasters. Laudatory reviews almost always come from abroad. Afterward I published *Walls*. It was the sum of a series of stylistic approaches, of a certain insecurity, of situations that I myself didn't know how to handle because I didn't have sufficient experience but that nevertheless gave me the measure of what could come to be my work as a poet. A few poems in that book helped me trace the path of future works, and I kept always in mind that each new book of an author has to overcome the last.

Then I wrote *The Poor*. There's one event I can't mention too often, and that was the death of my father. It brought me to a complete revision of my method of poetic composition. It helped me better identify myself with the social marginality from which I come. It allowed me to write poetry whose central proposition is that it be valid.

ALCARAVÁN: It's obvious how important "My Father" is in *The Poor*.

SOSA: Yes, it is. And it let me fashion other poems at that same level of quality. After a few years, you begin to see what you really have written, and you never stop feeling the terror that what you've made might be worth nothing. It's the terror of every artist: that his work might be worth nothing, that he might not have contributed to the dignification of man, which is one of the tasks of art. If not, why write? It's possible, I think, that a poem or a story could help civilize those who govern; that's why we need governors who read.

ALCARAVÁN: You've told us about the poets whose footsteps

you followed in at first, but, from then to now, which poets have you come to prefer?

SOSA: One changes lovers with time. Slowly, I left Darío, Molina and Nervo behind. I came into contact with the poetry of Neruda, Brecht, Miguel Hernández. And the world of César Vallejo slapped me in the face. All these poets constituted a stimulus, but always, above everything, the search for one's own personality is what's essential. You have to be authentic, and you have to do it by means of the culture of your people (a term that often has lent to confusion, above all when you hear it from the lips of those who depreciate the people, from that sinister zoology that sets itself against the people).

I've also been influenced by Paul Eluard, Franz Kafka, and Giovanni Papini, who was the principal detonator of my passion for art. And, of course, the life I have lived and observed, the best of all my teachers.

* * *

(The poems of The Difficult Days are taken from The Poor and A World For All Divided.)

THE DIFFICULT DAYS

Esta Luz Que Subscribo

Esto que escribo
nace
de mis viajes a las inmovilidades del pasado. De la
   seducción
que me causa la ondulación del fuego
igual
que a los primeros hombres que lo vieron y lo sometieron
a la mansedumbre de una lámpara. De la fuente
en donde la muerte encontró el secreto de su eterna
   juventud.

De conmoverme
por los cortísimos gritos decapitados
que emiten los animales endebles a medio morir. Del amor
   consumado.
Desde la misma lástima, me viene.

Del hielo que circula por las oscuridades
que ciertas personas echan por la boca sobre mi nombre.
   Del centro
del escarnio y de la indignación. Desde la circunstancia
de mi gran compromiso, vive como es posible
esta luz que suscribo.

This Light I Subscribe To

What I'm writing
is born
of my trips to the past, and what is fixed there. Of the
   seduction

worked on me by shimmering fire
as it was worked
on the first men who saw fire and subdued it
to the meekness of a lamp. Of the fountain
where death found the secret of its eternal youth.

Of letting myself be moved
by the brief, beheaded screams
weak animals emit when halfway dead. Of consummate
   love.
Of grief, finally, all of the same grief.

Of the ice circulating through the darknesses
certain persons spew over my name. Of mockery
and indignation, at the quick. From the circumstance
of my great compromise, it lives as it may,
this light I subscribe to.

Los Pobres

Los pobres son muchos
y por eso
es imposible olvidarlos.

Seguramente
ven
en los amaneceres
múltiples edificios
donde ellos
quisieran habitar con sus hijos.

Pueden
llevar en hombros
el féretro de una estrella.
Pueden
destruir el aire como aves furiosas,
nublar el sol.

Pero desconociendo sus tesoros
entran y salen por espejos de sangre;
caminan y mueren despacio.

Por eso
es imposible olvidarlos.

The Poor

The poor are many.
That's why
we cannot forget them.

Surely
they see
in the morning light
many buildings
they would like
to live in with their children.

They can
shoulder
the coffin of a star.
They can
rip up the air like furious birds,
blot out the sun.

But not knowing their treasures
they enter and leave by mirrors of blood;
they walk, and die, slowly.

That's why
we cannot forget them.

Transparencia

Los hospitales
asignados a las pobres gentes
encierran
las amplitudes de los dobles fondos.

Allí los médicos penetran
los confines de los desválidos
y escuchan la tristeza dentro de una caja iluminada.

En los días de lluvia
los enfermos mentales
imaginan lagunas y veleros;
navegan al olvido y ya no vuelven.

En los pasillos, monjas y sacerdotes
detrás
de la espesura de sus hábitos,
cruzan frases,
cambian inclinaciones,
descienden las escalas de encantados ramajes.

Los pacientes se pasan las horas
midiendo la brevedad de la existencia;
o admirando
las enfermeras
con pechos protegidos por los dedos de lo tierno

La muerte
acostada en los anfiteatros
envía la inmovilidad de su amenaza.

Cualquiera
puede hacer suyas estas palabras
un día de visitas,
un jueves, por ejemplo.

Transparency

The hospitals
assigned to the poor
are spacious
as trunks with false bottoms.

Doctors there force
the last doors of the helpless
and listen to sadness in a lighted box.

On rainy days
the mentally ill
imagine lagoons, and boats there with sails.
They sail out to oblivion and no longer return.

In the corridors, nuns and priests
beneath
the heaviness of their habits
exchange small talk,
bow to each other,
descend enchanted arbors step by step.

Patients pass the hours
measuring the briefness of their existence
or admiring
the nurses
with breasts shielded by the fingers of tenderness.

Death
lounging on the dissecting tables
extends his open invitation.

Anyone
can make these words his
any visitor's day,
a Thursday, for example.

Los Peldaños Que Faltan

Nuestros hijos
ven
la ruina acumulada de las ciudades.

Tocan el velo extendido en las barriadas.

Meditan
en los choques que producen las caídas
de las golondrinas
que ya no distinguen los hilos telegráficos

Se contemplan dentro del diario espejo sucio
que nadie advierte.

Aprenden con los moribundos
a contar los peldaños que faltan a la vida.
Y crecen sin asombro.

The Missing Stairs

Our children
see
the hoarded ruin of cities.

Touch the veil that laps the suburbs.

Muse
upon the shocks caused by the falling
of the swallows
that no longer distinguish the telegraph wires.

Contemplate themselves inside the daily dirty mirror
no one answers for.

Learn with the dying
to count life's missing stairs.
And grow up unamazed.

Los Indios

Los indios
bajan
por continuos laberintos
con su vacio a cuestas.

En el pasado
fueron guerreros sobre todas las cosas.
Levantaron columnas al fuego
y a las lluvias de puños negros
que someten los frutos a la tierra.

En los teatros de sus ciudades de colores
lucieron vestiduras
y diademas
y máscaras doradas
traídas de lejanos imperios enemigos.

Calcularon el tiempo
con precisión numérica.
Dieron de beber oro líquido
a sus conquistadores,
y entendieron el cielo
como una flor pequeña.

En nuestros días
aran y siembran el suelo
lo mismo que en edades primitivas.
Sus mujeres modelan las piedras del campo
y el barro, o tejen
mientras el viento
desordena sus duras cabelleras de diosas.

The Indians

The Indians
descend
maze after maze
with their emptiness on their backs.

In the past
they were warriors over all things.
They put up monuments to fire
and to the rains whose black fists
put the fruit in the earth.

In the theaters of their cities of colors
shone vestments
and crowns
and golden masks
brought from faraway enemy empires.

They marked time
with numerical precision.
They gave their conquerors
liquid gold to drink,
and grasped the heavens
like a tiny flower.

In our day
they plow and seed the ground
the same as in primitive times.
Their women shape clay
and the stones of the field, or weave
while the wind
disorders their long, coarse hair, like that of goddesses.

Los he visto sin zapatos y casi desnudos,
en grupos,
al cuidado de voces tendidas como látigos,
o borrachos balanceándose con los charcos del ocaso
de regreso a sus cabañas
situadas en el final de los olvidos.

Les he hablado en sus refugios
allá en los montes protegidos por ídolos
donde ellos son alegres como ciervos
pero quietos y hondos
como los prisioneros.

He sentido sus rostros
golpearme los ojos hasta la última luz,
y he descubierto así
que mi poder no tiene
ni validez ni fuerza.

Junto a sus pies
destruidos por todos los caminos,
dejo mi sangre
escrita en un oscuro ramo.

I've seen them barefoot and almost nude,
in groups,
guarded by voices poised like whips,
or drunk and wavering with the pools of the setting sun
on the way back to their shacks
in the last block of the forgotten.

I've talked with them up in their refuges
there in the mountains watched over by idols
where they are happy as deer
but quiet and deep
as prisoners.

I've felt their faces
beat my eyes until the dying light
and so have discovered
my strength is neither
sound nor strong.

Next to their feet
that all the roads destroyed
I leave my own blood
written on an obscure bough.

La Realidad

Llueve. Cruje
la realidad.

(En las grandes ciudades
los bosques
y las bellas armas de casa bajo la lluvia
son dos cuerpos hermosos.)

Algo
se rompe
dentro del hombre
que ha caminado demasiado solo.

Llueve. El espejo es idéntico.
Alguien me dice: es cierto,
nosotros no tenemos esperanza.

Reality

It's raining. Reality
rustles.

(In the great cities
the forests
and lovely housewives in the rain
are two voluptuous bodies.)

Something
breaks
inside the man
who has walked too alone.

It's raining. In the mirror too.
Someone says to me: it's true,
we have no hope.

La Yerba Cortada por los Campesinos

Cuántas veces nos ha parecido
que lo más importante de nuestras vidas
es el vuelo de las abejas que precede a las colegialas
que retornan de las aulas, pensando en nada,
felices como peces

Y cuántas veces hemos razonado
que la rebeldía contra un sistema de cosas
impuesto
a través
de asesinos alquilados
investidos
de infinitos poderes,
nos dignifica.

En nuestra segunda inocencia hemos imaginado
que alguien nos llama
desde un lugar hermoso parecido al mar, y que la voz
viene de la garganta de esa mujer delgada que esperamos en
    vano;
o que nos llama el amigo de infancia, aquel
cuyo padre comía tinieblas en los días difíciles.

Y cuántas veces al hablar de nuestra verdad
hemos creído
hablar de la verdad que interesa a las grandes mayorías,
y nos hemos sentido emocionados por ello porque sabemos
que el líquido de la verdad altera el pulso y envía una carga
no acostumbrada al corazón, que puede convertirse de este
    modo
en una suerte de Esfinge sin enigmas.

The Grass the Peasants Cut

How often it has seemed to us
that what is most important in our lives
is the flight of bees that comes before the coeds
fresh from the lecture halls, nothing on their minds,
content as fish.

And how often we have reasoned
that to rebel against a system
imposed
by means
of hired assassins
invested
with infinite powers
lends us dignity.

In our second innocence we've imagined
that someone is calling us
from a lovely place much like the sea, and that the voice
is from the throat of that slender woman we await in vain;
or that the childhood friend is calling us
whose father ate shadows in the difficult days.

And how often on speaking our truth
have we believed
we speak the truth the great majorities would like to hear,
how often been uplifted knowing
that the liquid of truth, that fires the pulse and sends
an unaccustomed charge through the veins, can change the
    heart
into a species of Sphinx without riddles.

Y así creemos vivir aproximándonos a lo perfecto.

En realidad
sólo
lo que hace el hombre
por enaltecer al hombre es trascendente.

La yerba cortada por los campesinos es igual a una
    constelación.
Una constelación es igual a una piedra preciosa,
pero el cansancio de los campesinos que cortaron la yerba
es superior al Universo.

Demostrar los hechos mezclados con las lentitudes
de un fuego que no conocemos, y quemar incienso a las
    buenas gentes,
ayuda a vivir,
ayuda a bien morir.

And so we think to live approaching what is perfect.

In reality
nothing
but what man does
to exalt man is transcendent.

The grass the peasants cut is equal to a constellation
and that constellation to a precious gem
but the weariness of the peasants who cut the grass
outweighs the Universe.

To unravel events intertwined with a slow-burning
fire that is not ours to know, and to burn incense to the
   good people,
helps to live,
helps to die well.

Los Elegidos de la Violencia

No es fácil reconocer la alegría
después de contener el llanto mucho tiempo.

El sonido de los balazos
puede encontrar de súbito
el sitio de la intimidad. El cielo aterroriza
con sus cuencas vacías. Los pájaros pueden alojar la
    delgadez
de la violencia entre patas y pico. La guerra fría
tiende su mano azul y mata.

La niñez, aquella de los cuidados cabellos de vidrio,
no la hemos conocido. Nosotros nunca hemos sido niños.
El horror
asumió su papel de padre frío. Conocemos su fuerza
con lentitud de asfixia. Conocemos su rostro
línea por línea,
gesto por gesto,
cólera por cólera. Y aunque desde las colinas admiramos el
    mar
tendido en la maleza, adolescente el blanco oleaje,
nuestra niñez se destrozó en la trampa
que prepararon nuestros mayores.

Hace ya muchos años
la alegría
se quebró el pie derecho y un hombro,
y posiblemente ya no se levante,
la pobre.

Mirad.
Miradla cuidadosamente.

Those the Violence Selects

It's not easy to recognize joy
after holding back tears a long time.

The sound of gunfire
can go straight to the heart
of our intimacy. The sky terrifies
with its empty sockets. Birds can lodge the lean figure
of violence between beak and claw. The cold war
flexes its blue hand and kills.

Childhood, the one of the pampered glass hairs,
we never knew. We have never been children.
Horror
assumed its role as the frigid father. We came to know his
    strength

as it strangled us, slowly, and his face
line by line
look by look
fury by fury. And although from the hills we admired the
    sea
sprawled on the weedy shore, and the waves in their white
    adolescence,
our childhood perished in an ambush
set by our elders.

Many years ago now
joy
broke its right foot and a shoulder
and now may not get up,
poor thing.

Look at it.
Look at it carefully.

Las Voces No Escuchadas de
los Ricos

Somos y hemos sido los mismos.

Nunca sabemos
lo que necesitamos de este mundo,
pero
tenemos sed—mar de extremos dorados—el agua
no se diferencia
de una muchedumbre
extraviada
dentro de un espejismo.

Hemos quebrado a los más fuertes.
Hemos enterrado a los débiles en las nubes.
Hermos inclinado la balanza del lado de la noche,
y a pesar de los azotes recibidos
permanecemos en el templo.

Muy pocos
entienden
el laberinto de nuestro sueño.

Y somos uno.

Unheard Voices of the Rich

We are and we have been the same.

We never know
what we need from this world
but
sea of golden crests, we thirst, and the water
is no different
than a multitude
estranged
inside a mirage.

We have broken the strongest.
The weak we have buried in clouds.
The scales we have tipped to the side of the night
and in spite of the whip
we remain in the temple.

Few
fathom
the labyrinth of our dream.

And we are one.

La Muerte Otra

Ellos, los enemigos nuestros de cada día,
vendrán inesperadamente.
Tres veces llamarán con firmes golpes. Tengo
el presentimiento del eco duplicado
de sus pasos
calmados.

(Pesan en el ambiente las desgracias, olfateadas
por los perros del barrio, empujados al fondo,
íngrimos,
llenos de agua los ojos.)

Son ellos, los enviados que se abren brutalmente,
los desiguales
distribuidores
de la muerte inventada que pasan en silencio,
y que un día vendrán.

Mi mujer extrañará los arcos de mis nervios
y mis hijos se inquietarán, enmudecidos,
por la idea de la humedad, y por la suerte
de las aves soledosas paradas en los vétices.

The Other Death

Our everyday enemies, they
will come unexpectedly
and knock three times, each time firmly. I hear it
now, already, in the duplicate echo
of their calm,
unhurried steps.

(The air is heavy with miseries, miseries sniffed
by the neighborhood dogs, miseries shoved to the
    background,
loners,
their eyes full of tears.)

They are the ones, the messengers of brutal confidences,
the unequal
distributors
of fabricated death, who pass in silence
and who one day will come.

My wife will wonder at my nervousness
and my children will fret, mutely,
at the hint of dampness, and because of the sort
of solitary birds perched on top of their heads.

Los Claustros

Nuestros cazadores
—casi nuestros amigos—
nos han enseñado, sin equivocarse jamás,
los diferentes ritmos
que conducen al miedo.

Nos han amaestrado con sutileza.
Hablamos,
leemos y escribimos sobre la claridad.
Admiramos sus sombras
que aparecen de pronto.
Oímos
los sonidos de los cuernos
mezclados
con los ruidos suplicantes del océano.

Sin embargo
sabemos que somos los animales
con guirnaldas de horror en el cuerpo;
los cercenados a sangre fría; los que se han dormido
en un museo de cera
vigilado
por maniquíes de metal violento.

The Sanctuary

They are almost our friends
who are hunting us now
never missing a beat
while they teach us the various rhythms
for running in fear.

The training has been subtle.
We speak
read and write about illumination
then applaud as their shadows
pop up on the spot.
We hear
the sounding of the horns
blend
with the begging noises of the sea.

Nevertheless
we know we are the animals
whose bodies bear garlands of horror,
whose heads were lopped off in cold blood, who have slept
in a wax museum
where the watch is kept
by mannequins of murderous steel.

La Hora Baja

Eran los años primeros.
Cruzábamos entonces la existencia
entre
lineales zumbidos,
difuntos calumniados
y ríos poseedores de márgenes secretas. Eramos
los vagabundos hermanos
de los canes sin dueño,
cazadores de insectos,
jurados enemigos
de torpes
implacables policías;
guerreros inmortales
de la mitología no distinguíamos un ala
del cuerpo de una niña.

Dando vueltas y cambios crecimos duramente.

De nosotros
se levantaron
los jueces de dos caras; los perseguidores
de cien ojos, veloces en la bruma y alegres
consumidores de distancias; los delatores fáciles;
los verdugos sedientos de púrpura; los falsos testigos
creadores de la gráfica del humo; los pacientes
hacedores
de nocturnos cuchillos.

Algunos dijeron: es el destino
que nos fue asignado, y huyeron
dejando la noche enterrada. Otros
prefirieron encerrarse entre cuatro paredes sin principio ni
fin.

Low Hour

They were the first years.
We crossed existence then
between
the paths of ricochets,
slandered corpses
and rivers with undisclosed sources and mouths. We were
the vagabond brothers
of ownerless hounds,
hunters of insects,
sworn enemies
of slow
implacable policemen.
Immortal warriors
of myth, we made no distinctions. A wing,
the body of a baby girl, to us were all the same.

Turning and changing we grew up tough.

From us
arose
the two-faced judges; the hundred-eyed
pursuers, swift in the fog, gladly
gulping down the miles; the willing informers;
executioners with a taste for the wine in a vein; the false
    witnesses
who first diagrammed smoke; the knifemakers
who work night after night
and never tire.

Some of them said: it's the destiny
assigned us, and then fled
leaving night in its grave. Others
preferred to shut themselves inside four walls without a
    door.

Pero todos nosotros—a cierta hora—recorremos
la callejuela de nuestro pasado
de donde
volvemos
con los cabellos tintos en sangre.

But we all—at a certain hour—go back by
the back streets of our past
and from there
return
with our hair dyed in blood.

Malignos Bailarines sin Cabeza

Aquellos de nosotros
que siendo hijos y nietos
de honestísimos hombres del campo,
cien veces
negaron sus orígenes
antes y después
del canto de los gallos.
Aquellos de nosotros
que aprendieron de los lobos
las vueltas
sombrías
del aullido y el acecho,
y que a las crueldades adquiridas
agregaron
los refinamientos de la perversidad
extraídos
de las cavidades de los lamentos.
Y aquellos de nosotros
que compartieron (y comparten)
la mesa
y el lecho
con heladas bestias velludas destructoras
de la imagen de la patria, y que mintieron o callaron
a la hora de la verdad, vosotros,
—solamente vosotros, malignos bailarines sin cabeza—
un día valdréis menos que una botella quebrada
arrojada
al fondo de un cráter de la Luna.

Wicked Headless Dancers ·

Those of us
· who, being sons and nephews
of most honorable countrymen,
a hundred times
denied their roots
before and since
the crowing of the cocks.
Those of us
who learned from wolves
the shady
stunts
of howl and ambush
and who to acquired cruelties
affixed
perverse refinements
quarried
from the mines of sorrow.
And those of us
who shared (and share)
their bed
and board
with frigid shaggy beasts, destroyers
of our country's image, and who lied or kept silent
at the moment of truth, you
—just you, wicked headless dancers—
one day will be worth less than a broken bottle
tossed
to the bottom of a crater of the Moon.

Las Sales Enigmáticas

Los Generales compran, interpretan y reparten
la palabra y el silencio.

Son rígidos y firmes
como las negras alturas pavorosas. Sus mansiones
ocupan
dos terceras partes de sangre y una de soledad,
y desde allí, sin hacer movimientos, gobiernan
los hilos
anudados a sensibilísimos mastines
con dentaduras de oro y humana apariencia, y combinan,
nadie lo ignora, las sales enigmáticas
de la *orden superior*, mientras se hinchan
sus inaudibles anillos poderosos.

Los Generales son dueños y señores
de códigos, vidas y haciendas, y miembros respetados
de la Santa Iglesia Católica, Apostólica y Romana.

The Mysterious Sallies

The Generals buy, interpret and divide
the silence and the word.

As stern and absolute
as heaven, and as dreadful and black, they are. Their
  mansions
take up
two parts blood and one part solitude
and from there, apparently immobile, they pull
strings
attached to nervous mastiffs
with gold dentures and the human look, and so pull off,
it's common knowledge, mysterious sallies
of the *highest order*, while their mute
rings of power hum and swell.

The Generals are gentlemen, possessors
of codes, lives and houses, and respectable members
of the Holy Catholic Church, Roman and Apostolic.

Piano Vacío

Si acaso
deciden
buscarme,
me encontrarán
afinando mi caja de música.

Podrán
oír entonces
la canción que he repetido
a boca de los anocheceres: *ustedes*
destruyeron
cuidadosamente
mi patria y escribieron su nombre en libros secretos.
A nosotros
nos transformaron en espantapájaros.

Si acaso
deciden
buscarme
estaré esperándoles
junto a mi silencio de piano vacío.

Empty Piano

If by chance
they decide
to look me up,
they'll find me
tuning my music box.

They'll be able,
then, to hear
the song I sing again
as each night falls: *it's you*
who've carefully
destroyed
my country, and forged her name in secret books.
As for us
you've turned us into scarecrows.

If by chance
they decide
to look me up,
I'll be waiting for them
next to the silence of my empty piano.

La Batalla Oscura

He vuelto.
El caserío se desploma y flota su nombre
solamente.

Beso la tarde como quien besa una mujer dormida.

Los amigos
se acercan con un rumor de infancia en cada frase.

Las muchachas
pronuncian mi nombre y yo admiro sus bocas con animal
  ternura.

Levanto una piedra quien alza un ramo
sin otro afán que la amistad segura.

La realidad sonríe
tal vez
porque
algo
he inventado en esta historia. He vuelto, es cierto,
pero nadie me mira ni me habla, y si lo hacen,
escucho una batalla de palabras oscuras entre dientes.

(Las brasas del hogar amplían los rincones
y doran las tijeras del día que se cierra.)

Un esfuerzo violáceo
contiene mi garganta.

The Dark War

I'm back.
The village collapses and leaves afloat
only its name.

I kiss the afternoon as one would kiss a woman sleeping.

Friends
come up and say the things it seems a child would say.

Girls
utter my name and I admire their mouths with` an animal
  tenderness.

I pick up a rock as one would grasp a branch,
wanting nothing more than certain friendship.

Reality smiles
perhaps
because
something
in this story is my own invention. I'm back, that's true,
but no one looks at me or speaks to me, and if they do
all I hear is a war of dark words in their teeth.

(The coals of the hearth push back the corners
and gild the closing scissors of the day.)

A spirit the color of violets
stops my song in its throat.

Mi Padre

I

De allá de Cuscatlán de sur anclado
vino mi padre
con despeñados lagos en los dedos.

El conoció lo dulce del límite que llama.
Amaba los inviernos,
la mañana,
las olas.

Trabajó sin palabras
por darnos pan y libros
y así jugó a los naipes vacilantes del hambre.

No sé cómo en su pecho
se sostenía un astro
ni cómo lo cuidó de las pedradas.

Sólo sé que esta tierra
constructora de pinos
le humilló simplemente.

Por eso se alejaba
(de música orillado)
hacia donde se astillan crepúsculo y velero.

Miradle, sí, miradle
que trae para el hijo
gaviota
y redes de aire.

Mi puerta toca y dice: *buenos días*.
Miradle, sí, miradle
que viene ensangrentado.

My Father

I

From beyond Cuscatlán, my father came.
The south was his anchor.
In his fingers were lakes that had leapt to their death.

He knew the sweetness of the summoning horizon.
He loved winters,
morning,
waves.

He worked without words
to give us bread and books.
It was his way of dealing hunger's stacked deck.

I don't know how
he kept a star alive inside his breast
nor how he shielded it from stonings,

I know only that this earth
assembler of pines
absolutely humbled him.

That's why he left behind
his landfall—music—
for where dusk and the sailboat collide.

Look at him, yes, look at him
who brings his son
seagulls
and nets made of air.

He knocks at my door and says: *good morning.*
Look at him, yes, look at him,
coming here all covered with blood.

Después
los hospitales
y médicos inmensos vigilando la escarcha.
Su traje y desamparo combatiendo el espanto.
Sus pulmones azules,
la poesía
y mi nada.

Un día sin principio cayó en absurda yerba.

Su brazo campesino
borró espejos
y rostros
y chozas
y comarcas;
y los trenes del tiempo
en humo inalcanzable se llevaron su nombre.

Nueve le dimos tierra.
Aún oigo los pasos
de asfalto,
ruina y viento.
Las campanas huyendo
y el golpe de la caja que derribó el ocaso.

Yo no hubiera querido regresarme
y dejarle inmensamente solo.

Frente al agua del agua,
padre mío,
¿qué límites te llaman?

Mi niño bueno, dime,
¿qué mano pudo hacerlo?

Afterwards
the hospitals
and huge doctors watching over the frost.
His gown and his helplessness fighting the terror.
His blue lungs,
poetry
and my nothing.

On a day with no dawn, he fell in the farcical weeds.

His field hand's arm
wiped out mirrors
and faces
and shanties
and borders
and the railroads of time
have hauled off his name
in unreachable smoke.

Nine of us laid him to rest.
I hear our footsteps still
on the asphalt,
in ruin and the wind,
hear still the fleeting bells
and the box hitting bottom and smashing the sunset.

I wouldn't have wanted to go home
and leave him so immensely alone.

Facing the water of waters,
Father,
what horizons call?

Tell me, my good boy,
what hand could have done it?

Dejadle.
Así dejadle: que nadie ya le toque.

II

Quien creó la existencia
calculó la medida del sepulcro.
Quien hizo la fortuna hizo la ruina.
Quien anudó los lazos del amor
dispuso las espinas.

El astro no descubre su destello.
Ignora el pez el círculo del astro.
Se halla solo el viajero
en su deseo
de llegar a la cruz del horizonte.

Es lenta la partida y el sendero lento.
La luz
se borra en la extensión
y el universo en lo que no se sabe.

Caen las rotas hojas de los árboles.
El hombre—maniatado en sus orígenes—
se encamina
hacia un claustro sin llave ni salida.

Mi padre
tenía la delgadez en sombra
del cristal en el pecho;
cuando hablaba, a la hora de la espesura,
se volvían sus labios inmortales.

Sin su decidida bondad
no existiría
para mí esa calma y su ojo de pájaro en reposo.
La pobreza sería una divinidad indigna.

Leave him.
Let him be. No one touch him now.

II

Who ordered life
laid out the grave.
Who spawned fortune sired ruin.
Who tied the knots of love   ·
knit in the thorns.

The star hides in its glow.
The fish ignores the orbit of the star.
The traveler desiring
to cross the horizon
will find himself alone.

The leaving is slow and the traveling slow.
Light
fades in its unfolding
and the universe in what is unknown.

Torn leaves slip from the trees.
Man—handcuffed to his origins—
is headed
for a cell with no key, no way out.

My father
was slender
as the crystal pendant at a woman's breast.
When he spoke, in noon's thick heat,
his lips lived forever.

If not for his unflagging kindness,
that tranquility and his eye like a roosting bird's
would not exist for me.
Poverty would be a vile divinity.

45

Alegraré lo triste de los días.
Seré un grano de arena o una yerba.
Saludaré
como antes
las arañas de luces que cuelgan de la esfera
todo ello
para tocar sus hombros,
porque,
¿qué hubiera sido de mí, niño como era,
de no haber recibido
la rosa diaria
que él tejía con su hilo más tierno?

Vienen a mi memoria
sin que pueda evitarlo
las ciudadelas que recorrimos juntos;
el griterío de la gente
ante la pólvora y sus golpes en el aire;
los íconos custodiados de cerca
por la astucia de los frailes de pueblo.
O los sucesos de aquel puerto: el mar, me acuerdo,
vestido de negro, abandonó la orilla.
Al fondo
se erguía la presencia del hielo, martillo en alto;
en ese entonces, padre,
padeciste en tu carne
el dolor del planeta.

El agua
ha dispuesto
sus muebles de lujo en el césped.
Los frutos están bajos para todas las bocas.
El estaría ahora tratando de alcanzarlos
reflejados en el río. O vendría a buscarme
y me diría: *no me dejes. Soy un viejo ya.*
Tienes que volver a mi lado. Ayer

Sorrow of days, I will make you happy.
I will be a grain of sand or a weed.
I will welcome
as a child
the brilliant chandeliers that hang from heaven.
All that
just so I can touch his shoulders
because,
young as I was, what would have become of me
if I hadn't received
the daily rose
he wove with his tenderest thread?

To my memory
irresistibly
come the forts we visited together,
the shouting of crowds
at fireworks bursting in the air,
the icons closely guarded
by cautious village friars.
Or what happened in that port: the sea,
dressed in mourning, deserted the shore.
From the mud up
the ice swelled with pride, hammer held high.
In that time, Father,
the anguish of the whole earth
nested in your flesh.

The water
has arranged
its finest furniture on the lawn.
The fruits are low enough for every mouth.
He'd be trying to read them now, those
reflections in the river, or he'd come looking for me
to tell me: *don't leave me. I'm an old man now.*
You've got to stick by my side. Yesterday

escribí una carta a tu madre. Sabes,
cuando oigo los gritos
de los pájaros del lugar,
siento que algo
me une más a ella.

Caminaba
—doy mi testimonio—
del brazo de fantasmas
que lo llevaron a ninguna parte.
Caía
abandono abajo, cada vez más abajo,
más abajo,
con ayes sin sonido,
repitiendo ruidos no aprendidos,
buscando continuamente
el encuentro con los arrullos dentro de la apariencia.

Queda el eco en el muro.
Subsisten
los aullidos del ultrajado.
La sangre del cordero
no la limpia el curso de la fuente:
se adhiere en la piel de los verdugos,
y cuando ellos abren sus roperos,
surge su mano nunca concluida.

No.
Para ellos no habrá quietud posible.
El humo de las hogueras apagadas
eleva sus copas acusadoras.

En sus refugios hallarán un tiempo de duda;
en sus lechos
estará esperándoles
la rapidez del áspid.

I wrote a letter to your mother. You know,
when I hear the calling
of the birds around here,
I feel something
tie me closer to her.

He walked
—I testify to this—
arm in arm with phantoms
who led him nowhere.
He fell
deep into despair, each time deeper,
deeper,
silently consenting,
repeating rumors he knew nothing of,
incessantly seeking
an encounter with the lullabies inside what seems to be.

The echo remains in the wall.
The howls of the abused
live on.
The blood of the lamb
is not washed away by the spray of the fountain:
it sticks to the executioners' skin
and when they open their wardrobes
his hand, never done for, jumps out.

No.
For them there's no possible peace.
The smoke of smothered fires
lifts up its accusing cups.

In their hideouts they will find
a time of doubt. Between their sheets
will be awaiting them
the instant of the asp.

No.
Para ustedes
no habrá tregua
ni perdón.

En este mismo sitio
me habló de la ventisca
que azota sin descanso los asilos,
de su amor a los árboles en medio del silencio.

Hoy
que no vamos juntos
me siento entre descnocidos
que esquivan la mirada.

Hoy
que no está en mi mesa
compartiendo mi turbio vaso de agua
debe estar más solo de lo que imagino.

La lluvia en el cementerio
se convierte
en una catedral extraída de la plata.
Dentro, en los altares,
viudas de blanco
rezan cabizbajas.

Lejos
se oyen
las voces
de un coro que no existe.

Me llevas de la mano
como lo hacías antes.
Entramos en la única casa
que ha quedado en pie
después de la destrucción del día.

No.
For you
there will be neither pardon
nor truce.

On this very spot
he told me of the blizzard
that whips the asylums nonstop
and of his love for trees in silent groves.

Now
that we're no longer companions
everyone is strange
and looks away.

Now
that he's not here at my table
sharing water with me from a dirty glass
he must be unimaginably alone.

The rain in the graveyard
becomes
a spun silver cathedral.
Inside, at the altars,
widows in white
pray, heads bowed.

Far away
are heard
the voices
of a phantom choir.

You take me by the hand
the way you used to.
We enter the only house
still standing
since the day's destruction.

Cruzamos avenidas
que conducen a un mundo derrumbado.
Creemos escuchar una canción.
Volvemos: tú alto y yo pequeño,
pequeñito, para no hacerte daño.

Señalas la distancia.
Te quitas el pan de la boca
para salvarme un poco,
padre,
yo pienso que vives todavía.

De aquí partió y reposa bajo tierra.
Aún me duele el esfuerzo último de sus brazos.

We cross avenues
that lead to a lost world.
We think we listen to a song.
We turn back: you tall and I small,
tiny, to do you no harm.

You point out the distance.
You take the bread from your mouth
to save me a little.
Father,
I think you still live.

Here he left and lies under the ground.
The last effort of his arms aches within me still.

Arte Espacial

Llevo conmigo un abatido búho.

En los escombros levanté mi casa.
Dije
mi pensamiento a hombres de imágenes impúdicas.

En la extensión me inclino hecho paisaje, y siento,
vuelta música, la sombra de una amante sepultada.

Dentro de mí se abre el espacio
de un mundo para todos dividido.

Estos versos devuelven lo que ya he recibido:
un mar de fondo,
las curvas del anzuelo,
el coletazo de un pez ahogado en sangre,
los feroces silbidos enterrados, la forma
que adoptó la cuchillada, el terror congelado entre mis
    dedos.

Comprendo que la rosa no cabe en la escritura.

En una cuerda bailo hasta el amanecer
temiendo—cada instante—la breve melodía de un tropiezo.

Spatial Art

I keep a worn-out owl around.

Over the refuse I raised up my house.
I said
what I thought to the shameless faces.

Turned landscape I lean into space, and I feel,
become music, the shadow of a buried lover.

A new world opens up inside me,
one divided for all.

What I've received so far these verses give back here:
an ocean's swell,
a fishhook's curves,
a slap from the tail of a fish drowned in blood,
a fierce buried hissing, the shape
the gash assumed, the fear frozen in between my fingers.

I understand the rose won't fit inside the written word.

I dance on a tightwire till dawn
dreading—every moment—the brief melody of a slip.

Canción para un Gato Muerto

Era casi de música. Todo el color del cielo
se anudaba a su cola.

Murió difícilmente.

Imploraba mi ayuda llamándome, carcomido por la
    sombra,
con sus verticales lucecitas felinas,
alejándose fijo entre la llovizna de la agonía.

Y fino hasta el abismo, para no herir a nadie
con el roce de sus despojos, el pobre animalito
murió a solas vaciado en la penumbra.

Song for a Dead Cat

It was almost musical. All the color of the sky
was knotted to its tail.

It died hard.

Consumed by the shadows, it called for my help, begging
with its bright little upright cat eyes,
receding fixed inside a mist of agony.

And genteel to the edge of the abyss, not to wound anyone
with its last throes, the poor little creature
died alone, exhausted in the half-light.

Testimonios

El que ya no se acuerda
del interior del lujo
porque
lo han ocultado
millares de caras hambrientas.

El que cree que aquella mujer
que abre las ventanas de su casa
tiene
diminutas lluvias en el cabello.

El que se equivocó de nación y de amigos,
y nada sabe,
y sólo entiende
que la verdad aniquila a sus adoradores
si se atreven a verla de frente.

El salvaje que habita en el fondo de las edades,
ese soy,
ante un tiempo acosado
que ve cercano el fin.

Testimonies

He who no longer remembers
the decor of plenty
because
of the thousands of hungering faces
that stand in the way.

He who believes that that woman
opening the windows of her house
has
tiny showers in her hair.

He who was wrong about country and friends
and knows nothing
and understands only
that truth devours her lovers
if they dare to look her in the eye.

The savage who squats in the pit of the ages,
I am,
who watches a time under siege
near its end.

Los Días Difíciles

De joven creía que podía morir y renacer
de mis propios despojos.

Es una larga historia.

Fui marinero de la medianoche. Escalé montañas
con un cadáver atado a un tobillo. Falsifiqué mi efigie
a cambio de un plato de bellas falsedades. Fijé
mi residencia en el lado oculto de la realidad. Allí viví
diez años cometiendo abominables crímenes: escribí
a favor de la insolencia de los poderosos, novios purísimos
de la barbarie y agrimensores de la oblicua eternidad; elogié
la suavidad de las manos pausadas
de los ladrones de bancos; asesiné—*por órdenes
    superiores*—
el jardín de mi hermano mayor, que era su único tesoro.
Defendí con mi vida
las creencias de los mercaderes, ensalcé sus burlas
    sangrientas
a lo desconocido y su espantosa alegría de monos
    superiores.
Yo era entonces muy joven y creía que podía caer de bruces
sin sufrir daño alguno. Creía que podía conservar
sosegada en hondura mi barba mitológica.

He envejecido.
Hoy avanzo con dificultad; es imposible no lastimar con mi
    peso
los seres frágiles que transitan bajo mis zapatos, por la falta
de luz en mis ojos; mi camino está hecho de vasos
    estrellados,

The Difficult Days

As a boy I believed I could die and be born again
out of my very own ashes.

It's a long story.

I was a sailor of the midnight. I climbed mountains
with a corpse tied to one ankle, masked my face
for a dish of delicious deceits, settled
on the dark side of the real and lived there
ten years and committed unspeakable crimes: In print
I applauded contempt for the poor by the powerful,
    inhumanity's
virgin sweethearts, the surveyors of a biased eternity. I
    eulogized
the soft, sure hands
of the robbers of banks. I assassinated—*by command of my
    superiors*—
my elder brother's garden, the one treasure he had.
I defended the credo of merchants
with my life, and praised their bloody mockery
of the unknown, their terrifying joy superior among the
    apes.
I was still very young and believed I could fall on my face
for a laugh. I believed I could keep,
preserved in its gulf, my mythical beard.

Now I'm older.
Each step is an effort. There is so little light in my eyes, I
    can't help
but tread them under, the fragile souls that pass beneath
    my shoes.
My road is paved with shattered glasses,

falsas alarmas de incendios y ataques, telarañas
desordenadas
en los cuatro puntos cardinales cruzadas por ondulantes
miradas
(que adivino enemigas)
procedentes
de los bajos fondos,
en donde la poesía
se acuesta a dormir
y se levanta sumamente pálida, y en donde
el contacto
con una hoja
del nido de una víbora
puede matar.

false alarms of arson and invasions, spider webs strung
from the cardinal points and crosshatched with furtive
  glances
(I divine them enemical)
that issue
from the deepest of deeps
where poetry
lies down to rest
and rises ghostly pale, and where
a brush
with one leaf
from the nest of one viper
can kill.

Después de los Encuentros

Sobrevivo y envejezco.
Respiro
el aire quieto de las fotografías.

Cruzo puentes tendidos sobre dos oquedades.
Tropiezo
y caigo envuelto
en repentinos lazos
dispuestos
por algunos abogados de mirada podrida.

(Los rostros aumentan
o desaparecen
con absoluta falta de misterio.)

Hablo con campesinos,
con ocultos banqueros;
con mujeres rubias inclinadas en las flores.
Con poetas ya vencidos
por el vino y la noche
que cortan de un tajo la luna.

Veo en la ciudad un cuadro vacío.

Y advierto
lentamente
que se llena de plomo mi esqueleto.

After the Encounters

I live on, and grow old.
I inhale
the still air of photographs.

I cross bridges suspended over double hollows,
trip
and fall wrapped up
in hidden snares
staked out
by some corrupt-looking lawyers.

(Faces pile up
or disappear
with an absolute lack of mystery.)

I talk with countryfolk,
with cryptic bankers,
with blond women kneeling in the flowers.
With poets at last overcome
by wine and the night
who with one stroke fell the moon.

In the city I see a vacant block.

And it dawns on me
slowly
that my skeleton is filling with lead.

Un Anormal Volumen de Lluvia
(Crónica de un Juicio Final)

Ha llovido cien noches y cien días continuos
y la ciudad
ha sufrido
en sus ejes
un ángulo de inclinaciones
complicadísimas. Hoy, después de luchas inútiles,
amanecieron
absurdamente doblados
el señor Presidente de la República
y sus cercanos ayudantes: curas vigorosos,
diversos
invariables
dirigentes internacionales,
secretarias de espléndidas figuras y el vuelo
uniforme y quebradizo de ebrios buitres salvajes.

Adoptaron extrañas posiciones las mujeres
que se encontraban
tendidas con sus amantes
sobre la tierna maleza de los espejismos próximos a la
    aurora boreal;
la tristeza de la servidumbre
y la vaga amabilidad de los guardaespaldas,
de los prestamistas y de los agentes de seguros.

Se derrumbaron los pobres escritores honrados y los
    periodistas
con marcas infames y dolorosas en el rostro
hechas con tinta indeleble y los gánster retirados
    (fabricantes
de marcas) adictos
a las bebidas de colores sanguíneos
y expertos infalibles

An Unusual Amount of Rain
(A Doomsday Report)

It's rained a hundred days and nights now
and the city
has sustained
in its axis
a series of intricate
inclinations. Today, after futile resistance,
His Excellency The President of This Republic
awoke
absurdly warped
along with his close advisers: lusty priests,
various
invariable
world leaders,
shapely secretaries and a sickly but uniform flight
of hungover buzzards.

Strange positions had been assumed by the women
found
reclining with their lovers
on the soft, weedy bed of illusions by the aurora borealis—
that sadness of servants
and vague camaraderie of bodyguards,
pawnbrokers and insurance salesmen.

Swept away were the poor honored writers and the
    reporters
with the infamous, excruciating, indelible marks of their
    trade
on their faces; and the retired gangsters (makers
of trademarks), alcoholics
whose drinks were the color of blood
and infallible experts

en dédalos políticos y en las vacilaciones
y matices de la nube de la transfiguración
de la Banca.

Con los bultos de lluvia caídos
también se paralizaron los viajes
y se ensordecieron los instrumentos músicos.

on political entanglements and on the shifting
chameleon cloud of the transfiguration
of the Bank.

Because of the seemingly endless downpour
travel has also been paralyzed
and all musical instruments rendered tone-deaf.

Descripción de
una Ciudad en Peligro

Las cobras
han extraviado los únicos silbidos que poseían.

Las sirenas
silban
el nuevo día. Con fines inexplicables
los automóviles
trasladan
a puntos claves
inmensos sacos hinchados de silbidos.

La Prensa,
La Radio,
La T.V. y los Altos Círculos de la Nación
silban singularmente en circuito cerrado.

Los artistas, víctimas del lujo, a solas silban la poesía.

Los malhechores públicos convertidos en héroes
y en familias pudientes,
elevados
sobre grandes pedestales de hierro,
invisibles,
imponen, a fuego lento, la rueda alucinante de una moral
    silbada.

Con acento extranjero, tras gruesos lentes ahumados,
la policía
saca sombras chinas y desafinados silbidos de los huesos
de las víctimas elegidas. Las sábanas silban en los alambres
y la libertad silba en las ametralladoras, mientras,
reclinada en su lecho de rosas, la sífilis, con aire digno,
silba su monótona y dulzona y antigua canción.

Description of
an Endangered City

The cobras
have misplaced the only hisses they had.

Sirens
hiss in
the new day. Cars
and God knows why
are removing
to key points
immense sacks crammed with hisses.

The Press,
The Radio,
The T.V. and the High Circles of the Nation
hiss singularly in closed circuit.

The artists, victims of luxury, hiss poetry to themselves.

Public enemies turned heroes
with powerful families,
raised
on great iron pedestals,
invisible,
impose, over a slow fire, the dazzling wheel of a moral hiss.

With foreign accents, behind thick smoky lenses,
the police
pull china shadows and out-of-tune hisses from the bones
of their chosen victims. Sheets hiss in the wires
and liberty hisses in machine guns, while,
reclining in her bed of roses, syphilis, with a dignified air,
hisses her monotonous and syrupy and ancient song.

Las iluminaciones
superpuestas del teatro bifronte, los tenebrosos
    homosexuales
que flotan en dos aguas y los señoritos con aspecto de
    floreros;
el café
y las visitas intelectuales con un clavel de sospecha
en la solapa; la roja fotografía del bebedor y una cola
    infantil
que mueve al llanto, rechiflan
sus comedias
por el ojo insistente de una llave.

The superimposed illuminations
of the two-faced movie houses, nighttime homosexuals
who sail two seas and rich boys with the look of hothouse
   plants,
the cafe
and its intellectuals with the pink of suspicion
pinned to their lapels, the scarlet snapshot of the drinker
   and the childlike tail
that moves in time with tears, all
catcall their comedies
through a keyhole, a clamorous one.

El Aire Que Nos Queda

Sobre las salas y ventanas sombreadas de abandono.
Sobre la huida de la primavera, ayer mismo ahogada
en un vaso de agua.
Sobre la viejísima melancolía (tejida
y destejida largamente) hija
de las grandes traiciones hechas a nuestros padres y
    abuelos:
estamos solos.

Sobre las sensaciones de vacío bajo los pies.
Sobre los pasadizos inclinados
que el miedo y la duda edifican.
Sobre la tierra de nadie de la Historia: estamos solos,
sin mundo,
desnudo al rojo vivo el barro que nos cubre, estrecho
en sus dos lados el aire que nos queda todavía.

The Air We Have Left

Beyond the hallways and windows shadowed by neglect.
Beyond the flight of spring, drowned just yesterday
in a glass of water.
Beyond our age-old melancholy (loomed
and unraveled for so long) daughter
of the great betrayals of our fathers and theirs:
we are alone.

Beyond the feeling there is nothing underneath our feet.
Beyond the narrow passageways built
and tilted up by dread and doubt.
Beyond the no-man's land of History: we are alone,
without world,
the clay that covers us laid bare, the air still left us
narrow on both sides.

El Invierno Puede Ser un Inválido

Ya el invierno se ha ido.

Todo fue inútil, todo:
mi explicación de la noche
y sus fieras que no duermen,
mi grito.

Quizá se extravió en la escarcha,
o lo congeló el frío,
viejo y enfermo como iba.

Nadie lo sabe y es en vano
que yo trate de inquirirlo.

En un rincón de mi casa
veo aún la muleta
que olvidó.

Winter Can Be an Invalid

Winter's gone now.

It was all useless, all of it:
my explanation of the night
and its unsleeping fiends,
my scream.

He may have wandered off in the frost,
or frozen to death,
old and sick as he was.

Nobody knows. It's in vain
I try to find out about him.

In a corner of my house
I still see the crutch
he left behind.

La Arena del Desierto Que
Comparto con Otros

Unido a mis afectos, a sus bordes,
supongo
que conservo el horizonte,
las necesarias pausas de mi ritmo.

Cuento—sin un error, porque de la exactitud
depende mi vida—la arena del desierto
que comparto con otros en mi extraño té del atardecer.

Recibo
con ánimo cobarde la última noticia
sobre aquella amenaza
de la que nadie habla sin avergonzarse.

En vano trato de salvarme: la arena sube
justo
hasta el sitio del cuello.

De pie, teóricamente vivo, imagino que avanzo.

The Desert Sand I Share with Others

Bound to my affections, by their borders,
I suppose
I preserve the horizon,
the pauses necessary to my rhythm.

I count (without a slip, since on exactitude
my life depends) the desert sand
I share with others in my curious afternoon tea.

The latest news
concerns that threat
we're ashamed to discuss.
I feel weak in the knees.

In vain I try to save myself. The sand mounts
tight
around my collar.

On foot, theoretically alive, I imagine I am moving on.

THE LOCKERT LIBRARY
OF POETRY IN TRANSLATION

GEORGE SEFERIS: COLLECTED POEMS (1924-1955), translated, edited and introduced by Edmund Keeley and Philip Sherrard

COLLECTED POEMS OF LUCIO PICCOLO, translated and edited by Brian Swann and Ruth Feldman

C. P. CAVAFY: COLLECTED POEMS, translated by Edmund Keeley and Philip Sherrard and edited by George Savidis

BENNY ANDERSON: SELECTED POEMS, translated by Alexander Taylor

SELECTED POETRY OF ANDREA ZANZOTTO, translated and edited by Ruth Feldman and Brian Swann

POEMS OF RENE CHAR, translated by Mary Ann Caws and Jonathan Griffin

SELECTED POEMS OF TUDOR ARGHEZI, translated and edited by Michael Impey and Brian Swann

TADEUSZ ROZEWICZ: THE SURVIVOR, translated and introduced by Magnus J. Krynski and Robert Maguire

"HARSH WORLD" AND OTHER POEMS by Angel Gonzales, translated by Donald D. Walsh

DANTE'S "RIME," translated and introduced by Patrick S. Diehl

RITSOS IN PARENTHESES, translations and introductions by Edmund Keeley

SALAMANDER: SELECTED POEMS OF ROBERT MARTEAU, translated and introduced by Anne Winters

ANGELOS SIKELIANOS: SELECTED POEMS, translated and introduced by Edmund Keeley and Philip Sherrard

THE DAWN IS ALWAYS NEW: SELECTED POETRY OF ROCCO SCOTELLARO, translated by Ruth Feldman and Brian Swann

SELECTED LATER POEMS OF MARIE LUISE KASCHNITZ, translated by Lisel Mueller

OSIP MANDELSTAM'S "STONE," translated and introduced by Robert Tracy

THE MAN I PRETEND TO BE: "THE COLLOQUIES" AND SELECTED POEMS OF GUIDO GOZZANO, translated and edited by Michael Palma, with an introductory essay by Eugenio Montale

SOUNDS, FEELINGS, THOUGHTS: SEVENTY POEMS BY
WISŁAWA SZYMBORSKA, translated by Magnus J. Krynski and
Robert A. Maguire
D'APRES TOUT: POEMS BY JEAN FOLLAIN, translated and in-
troduced by Heather McHugh
SONGS OF SOMETHING ELSE by Gunnar Ekelöf, translated by
Leonard Nathan and James Larson
FUJIWARA NO SADAIE: THE LITTLE TREASURY OF ONE
HUNDRED PEOPLE, ONE POEM EACH, translated and an-
notated by Tom Galt
THE ELLIPSE: SELECTED POEMS OF LEONARDO SINISGALLI,
translated by W. S. Di Piero

Library of Congress Cataloging in Publication Data

Sosa, Roberto.
 The difficult days.

 (The Lockert library of poetry in translation)
 Selections in English and Spanish from Los pobres and Un mundo
para todos dividido.
 I. Lindsey, Jim, 1952-   . II. Sosa, Roberto. Mundo para todos
dividido. English & Spanish. Selections. 1983. III. Title. IV. Series.
PQ7509.2.S6A24   1983   861   83-42581
ISBN 0-691-06583-7
ISBN 0-691-01407-8 (pbk.)

Roberto Sosa is Professor of Literature at the University of Honduras.
Jim Lindsey is a translator and author of the book of poems, *In Lieu
of Mecca* (Pittsburgh).